Penguins

▲ Tammy Kennington

CHERRY LAKE
Publishing

Published in the United States of America by Cherry Lake Publishing
Ann Arbor, Michigan
www.cherrylakepublishing.com

Consultants: Dominique A. Didier, PhD, Associate Professor, Department of Biology, Millersville University;
Marla Conn, ReadAbility, Inc.
Book design: Sleeping Bear Press

Photo Credits: ©prochasson frederic/Shutterstock Images, cover, 1, 6; ©iStockphoto/Thinkstock, 5, 18; ©Stanislav
Fosenbauer/Shutterstock Images, 7; ©Neil Bradfield/Shutterstock Images, 9, 16; ©Dorling Kindersley RF/Thinkstock,
10; ©Christian Musat/Shutterstock Images, 11; ©Anton_Ivanov/Shutterstock Images, 12; ©pinguino k/ http://www.
flickr.com/ CC-BY-2.0, 13; ©Micha Klootwijk/Shutterstock Images, 15; ©Natalia Khalaman/Shutterstock Images, 17;
©Armin Rose/Shutterstock Images, 21; ©Rob Lilley/Shutterstock Images, 22; ©Guido Amrein, Switzerland/
Shutterstock Images, 24; ©Dmytro Pylypenko/Shutterstock Images, 27; ©fish1715/Shutterstock Images, 28

Library of Congress Cataloging-in-Publication Data

Kennington, Tammy, author.
Penguins / Tammy Kennington.
    pages cm. — (Exploring our oceans)
  Summary: "Discover facts about penguins, including physical features, habitat, life cycle, food,
and threats to these ocean creatures. Photos, captions, and keywords supplement the narrative of
this informational text"— Provided by publisher.
  Audience: 8-12.
  Audience: Grade 4 to 6.
  Includes bibliographical references and index.
  ISBN 978-1-62431-605-0 (hardcover) — ISBN 978-1-62431-617-3 (pbk.) —
ISBN 978-1-62431-629-6 (pdf) — ISBN 978-1-62431-641-8 (ebook)
  1. Penguins—Juvenile literature. I. Title.

  QL696.S47K46 2014
  598.47—dc23   2013032298

Cherry Lake Publishing would like to acknowledge the work of
The Partnership for 21st Century Skills. Please visit www.p21.org
for more information.

Printed in the United States of America
Corporate Graphics Inc.
January 2014

ABOUT THE AUTHOR

Tammy Kennington holds a bachelor's degree in elementary education and has earned certification
as a reading intervention specialist. She currently serves as a preschool director and tutors children
with dyslexia and related reading disorders. Tammy lives in Colorado Springs, Colorado, with her
husband and four children.

TABLE OF CONTENTS

CHAPTER 1

IN THE SWIM

You might have watched them dance or sing on the TV screen. Maybe you've read about their funny tricks in a children's book. Unlike Hollywood penguins, real penguins don't tap dance, use a toilet, or sleep in a bed.

Ocean explorer Ferdinand Magellan discovered penguins off the coast of Argentina in 1520. Describing the strange black birds, one passenger on the boat wrote that the birds could not fly and looked like "strange geese" with a "crow's beak." Magellan and his crew took several penguins and other unknown animals back to

Spain to learn more about them.

Penguins live in some of the coldest places on earth. The 18 species, or types, of penguins can be found on island beaches, volcanoes, and every continent in the **Southern Hemisphere**. Most penguins are social animals and live in large groups called **rookeries** or colonies.

Penguins live on land and in the water.

Penguins are called aquatic birds.

LOOK AGAIN

LOOK AT THE PENGUIN PICTURED HERE. WHAT DO YOU NOTICE ABOUT A PENGUIN'S BODY SHAPE THAT WOULD MAKE IT A GOOD SWIMMER?

Like other birds, penguins lay eggs and have feathers. They are warm-blooded animals, which means their body temperature stays almost the same all of the time. Unlike most birds, penguins do not fly. Instead, they spend up to 75 percent of their time hunting, diving, and swimming in the ocean. They can stay in the ocean for months at a time!

Ornithologists study birds and learn a lot about penguins from fossils. Penguin fossils show that at least 40 species of prehistoric penguins are now extinct. The largest extinct penguin was up to 5 feet 9 inches (175 cm) tall and weighed between 200 and 300 pounds (91 and 136 kg). Imagine a penguin as tall as an adult human!

The largest penguin alive today is the emperor penguin. The average emperor penguin is just over 3 feet 5 inches (104 cm) tall and weighs between 60 and 90 pounds (27 and 41 kg). At only 16 inches (40.6 cm) tall and less than 2.5 pounds (1 kg), the fairy penguin is smaller than most newborn babies. ⚓

Emperor penguins spend the winter on the open ice.

CHAPTER 2

BIRDS OF A FEATHER

Scientists believe that long, long ago, penguins could fly. Penguin bones used to be hollow like the bones of most birds. This meant the bones were light, making penguins better suited for flying. Today's penguins have heavy, dense bones. Heavy bones help penguins dive deep in the water. Also, penguins' wings have evolved into flippers for swimming.

Penguins have special feathers and skin that help them stay warm and dry. The feathers are made up of two parts. The first part is soft and fluffy. It provides warmth next to the penguin's skin. The second part of the feather is short and stiff. These small feathers connect to each other like pieces of a puzzle. It is difficult for cold water to reach the penguin's skin with thousands of feathers in the way. Like whales and seals, penguins have a layer of blubber, or fat, under their skin. **Blubber** also helps the birds stay warm even in cold temperatures.

Penguins spend most of their time in the water.

BODY DIAGRAM

eye

bill

flipper-like
wing

tail

webbed feet

claws

Emperor penguins are the largest living species of penguins.

Black and white **countershading** helps protect the penguin from predators when it's swimming. How? The bird's dark back blends into the ocean water when seen from above. Its stomach looks bright like the ocean's surface when seen from below. With such a clever disguise, hungry seals could swim past a penguin without knowing they just missed lunch.

Do you know of other sea creatures that have countershading?

Macaroni penguins have bright yellow feathers on their head and a strong, reddish colored beak.

The 18 species of penguins have a lot in common, but they have differences, too. The seven kinds of crested penguins have orange or yellow feathers above their eyes. With a black line running from one side of its chin to the other, the chinstrap penguin looks like it is wearing a bike helmet. The yellow-eyed penguin is named for its unusual eye color and has a row of yellow feathers across the top of its head.

This species of penguin lives all around Antarctica.

LOOK AGAIN

LOOK CLOSELY AT THIS PHOTOGRAPH.
CAN YOU DETERMINE WHAT KIND OF PENGUIN THIS IS?

CHAPTER 3

THE THRILL OF KRILL

Penguins are natural predators. They have good eyesight and use their flippers to move through the water. Penguins can flap their flippers up to 237 times in one dive. Their favorite food has a difficult time getting away.

Some species hunt together. Others look for food on their own. But all penguins like to eat food that lives in large groups. It makes mealtime much easier. Smaller penguins eat tiny shrimplike animals called **krill**. Bigger penguins enjoy squid and fish.

*Penguins are **carnivores**.*

Sometimes a penguin's diet depends on where it lives and which food is easiest to find. Because penguins eat up to 5 pounds (2.3 kg) of food every day, they spend a lot of time hunting. Penguins will often swim up to 4 miles (6.4 km) to find the catch of the day. The emperor penguin sometimes travels as far as 903 miles (1,453 km) in one hunting trip.

Most African penguins live along the southern coast of Africa.

Molting is a normal event for birds.

LOOK AGAIN

LOOK CLOSELY AT THIS PHOTOGRAPH OF A MOLTING PENGUIN. HOW WOULD YOU DESCRIBE THE WAY A MOLTING PENGUIN LOOKS COMPARED TO A PENGUIN THAT IS NOT MOLTING?

While penguins eat a lot, all penguins fast, or stop eating, twice each year. Penguins will fast when they begin to molt, or lose their old feathers. Old feathers are replaced by new, healthy ones. There are always enough feathers at one time to keep the penguin warm on land. But there are not enough to protect it from cold ocean water so they cannot hunt for food while molting. After two to four weeks of molting, the hungry penguins can hunt again.

The male emperor penguin protects an egg by holding it on top of his feet and covering it with a fold of skin.

[21ST CENTURY SKILLS LIBRARY]

The other time penguins fast is when they are breeding or taking care of their eggs. Some penguins fast for months. It depends on the species and whether the penguin is male or female. Some penguins take turns fasting. One parent will hunt for food while the other protects the eggs, then they trade places for a while. Most penguin parents, however, do not share the hard work of staying on land to care for their eggs. Instead, the mother leaves to hunt in the ocean while the father guards the eggs. The male emperor penguin has the longest fasting period. It can last up to four months.

CHAPTER 4

THE PENGUIN LIFE CYCLE

Penguins have interesting mating and nesting habits. Most breed every year in the spring or summer. But emperor penguins breed in the dark **Antarctic** winter when temperatures can be as low as -76 degrees Fahrenheit (-60 degrees Celsius). Scientists don't know why emperor penguins choose the coldest, windiest time of year to breed.

Courtship is a time when the male penguins try to impress the females. The work to win a mate begins with **trumpeting**. The male swings his head and struts

Penguins come out of the cold ocean water through a hole in the ice.

around an area he has chosen as a nest site. Then he calls out loudly and might flap his flippers to attract attention from the females. After he has a female's attention, both male and female penguins perform a type of dance. It is called a mutual display. Both penguins bob and stretch their necks while calling out noisily. The final stage of courtship is known as bowing. At least one of the penguins bends its beak toward the other bird's feet or the nest site.

Gentoo penguins make a lot of noise when trying to attract a mate.

Male penguins will sometimes offer small rocks or other nesting materials as gifts. The penguins will also groom or preen each other. Scientists think all of these activities help the pair recognize each other after a long time apart.

Together, the penguins build a nest made of pebbles, stones, plants, or form holes in the ground. One or two eggs are laid soon after the female chooses her mate. In order to hatch, the eggs must be kept warm. This process is called **incubation**. Some species take turns incubating the eggs, but the emperor penguin couple does not. The female rolls her only egg onto the male penguin's webbed feet and he tucks it under a roll of skin hanging from his stomach. The egg stays beneath the warm fold of skin for up to four months. During that time, the mother penguin hunts in the ocean. By the time she returns, the male has lost close to 50 percent of his body weight.

Newborn chicks are not prepared to care for themselves.

[21ST CENTURY SKILLS LIBRARY]

Once a chick is ready to hatch, it chips away at the shell with its beak. Hatching is difficult work and can take up to three days. When the chick hatches, it is covered by brown, black, white, or gray down.

Penguin chicks are not waterproof. They rely on their parents to hunt for food in the water. A penguin parent swallows and digests its catch. Then it **regurgitates** the food for the little penguin. Between 7 weeks and 14 months, the chick grows adult feathers. Then it can care for itself. If a chick survives until adulthood, it will probably live a total of 15 to 20 years.

GO DEEPER

WHAT IS THE MAIN IDEA OF THIS PARAGRAPH? PROVIDE ONE POINT THAT SUPPORTS THIS.

CHAPTER 5

PENGUINS AT RISK

Some penguin populations have as many as 11 million pairs. But there are fewer than 15,000 Galapagos penguins altogether. The International Union for Conservation of Nature classifies the African, erect-crested, Galapagos, northern rockhopper, and yellow-eyed penguins as **Endangered** on its Red List of Threatened Species. This means that populations have a very high risk of becoming **extinct**.

Why are these birds at risk for survival? Penguins have probably been a source of food for people for

Penguin nests can be made of small stones and pebbles.

centuries. In the 1800s, explorers, fishermen, and whale hunters began eating large numbers of penguins and their eggs. Some historians claim that more than 300,000 penguin eggs were taken from penguin colonies in Africa every year. With only one or two eggs in each nest, few chicks would live to be adults.

At the same time, penguin skins and feathers became an important part of the fashion world. Skins were made into slippers or purses, and feathers were perched on hats.

Environmental groups rescue animals and clean beaches like this that have been contaminated by oil spills.

People also removed oil from penguin blubber. Oil was hard to find and very important in the 1800s and early 1900s. It served as fuel and as a source of light.

Today, penguins still face dangers from humans. Oil spills can be deadly to penguins. When these birds are trapped in oil, their feathers are not fully waterproof. The penguins can die from cold or are poisoned when they preen their feathers.

Penguins must deal with predators, too. The penguin's ocean enemies are leopard seals, whales, and sharks. On land, penguins sometimes struggle with seabirds that threaten eggs and young chicks. Dogs, ferrets, snakes, and pigs also prey on penguins. In places like New Zealand, these animals have harmed the penguin population.

While penguin populations are struggling, people are taking action to protect them. Every species of penguin is legally protected. This means that no one is allowed to hunt penguins or collect their eggs.

THINK ABOUT IT

WHAT MAIN IDEA DOES THE AUTHOR EXPRESS IN THIS CHAPTER? SUPPORT YOUR ANSWER USING THE TEXT AND PHOTOGRAPHS.

THINK ABOUT IT

- After reading chapter 2, can you explain why penguins don't fly?

- Write three questions about penguins. Discuss them with a partner or in a small group.

- Read chapter 4 again. Compare and contrast the breeding and incubation habits of different penguins. What do you think is most interesting about penguin families? What else would you like to know?

- Read chapter 5 again. Do you think it is important to protect penguins? Why or why not?

LEARN MORE

FURTHER READING

Marzollo, Jean, and Laura Regan, illus. *Pierre the Penguin*. Ann Arbor, MI: Sleeping Bear Press, 2010.

Osborne, Mary Pope, Natalie Pope Boyce, and Sal Murdocca, illus. *Penguins and Antarctica: A Nonfiction Companion to Eve of the Emperor Penguins*. New York: Random House, 2008.

Schreiber, Anne. *Penguins!* Washington, DC: National Geographic, 2009.

WEB SITES

DLTK: Kid Zone—Penguins
www.kidzone.ws/animals/penguins/index.htm
Find activities, facts, and photos about penguins.

National Geographic Kids—Emperor Penguins
http://kids.nationalgeographic.com/kids/animals/creaturefeature/emperor-penguin
Watch a video of emperor penguins and read more about them.

Sea World: Animal Infobooks—Penguins
http://www.seaworld.org/animal-info/info-books/penguin

GLOSSARY

Antarctic (ant-AHRK-tik) the area close to or on the South Pole

blubber (BLUHB-er) fat layer found between the skin and muscles of a penguin

carnivores (KAHR-nuh-vorz) animals that eat other animals

countershading (KOUN-tur-shay-ding) the light and dark coloring of an animal to help it blend into its surroundings

endangered (en-DAYN-jurd) at risk of becoming extinct or of dying out

extinct (ik-STINGKT) no longer found alive

incubation (in-kyuh-BEY-shuhn) a period of time when eggs are kept warm so they will develop

krill (KRILL) small shrimplike animals

ornithologists (awr-nuh-THOL-uh-jists) scientists who study birds

regurgitates (ri-GUR-ji-tayts) throwing up digested food to share

rookeries (ROOK-uh-reez) places on land where birds gather in large groups

Southern Hemisphere (SUH-thurn HEM-i-sfeer) the half of the earth that is south of the equator

trumpeting (TRUHM-pit-eng) crying out loudly

INDEX